Dedicated to Ryan, Jeremy, Nathan and all of the athletes at Elite Camps.

Text & illustration copyright © 2024 by Stephanie Rudnick. All rights reserved.
Junk Food Baller by Stephanie Rudnick.
Published by Sport Lessons Press
https://lilballerbooks.com/

No part of this publication may be reproduced in whole or in part, or stored in a retrieval system, or transmitted in any form or by any means, electronic, mechanical, photocopying, recording, or otherwise, without written permission of the publisher/ author.
For information regarding permission, write to steph@lilballerbooks.com

ISBN # 978-1-998463-01-5

In the sunny town of Hoopville lived a little basketball player named Junk Food Baller.

Junk Food Baller had a big dream to become the best basketball player on the school team!

Every day, Junk Food Baller would head to the basketball court with his friends.

While his friends warmed up before they scrimmaged by dribbling and shooting, Junk Food Baller would munch on chips and candy, thinking it would fuel his game.

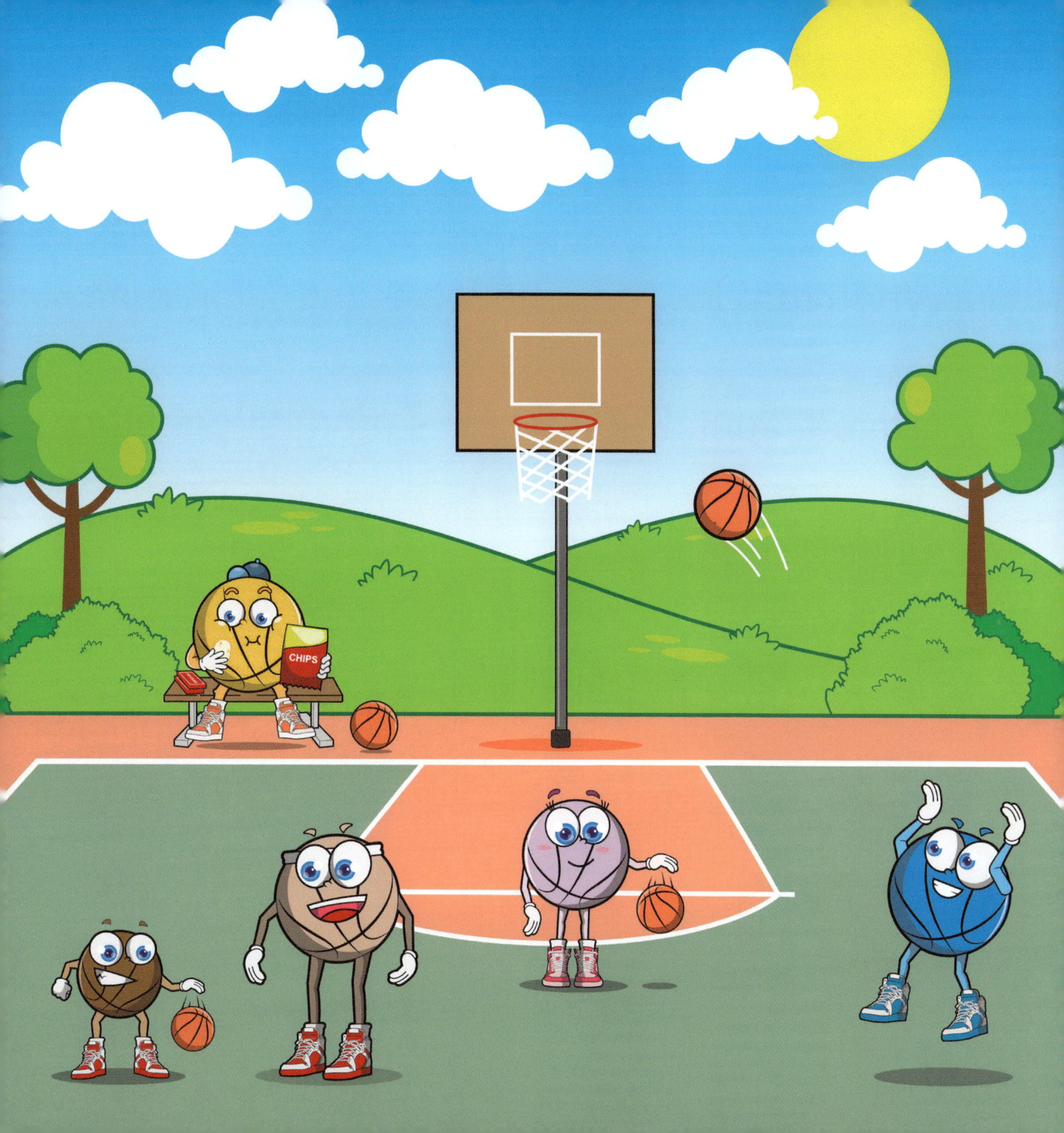
CHIPS

When the day for school basketball tryouts arrived, Junk Food Baller's mom suggested eating a healthy breakfast for energy.

But Junk Food Baller shook his head no, saying he preferred his sugar puff cereal.

SUGAR
PUFFS

In the locker room, the ballers were getting ready for the try-out.

Junk Food Baller grabbed a chocolate bar from his bag and started eating it.

His friend asked if that would give him a stomach ache. Junk Food Baller shook his head and said he needed the energy.

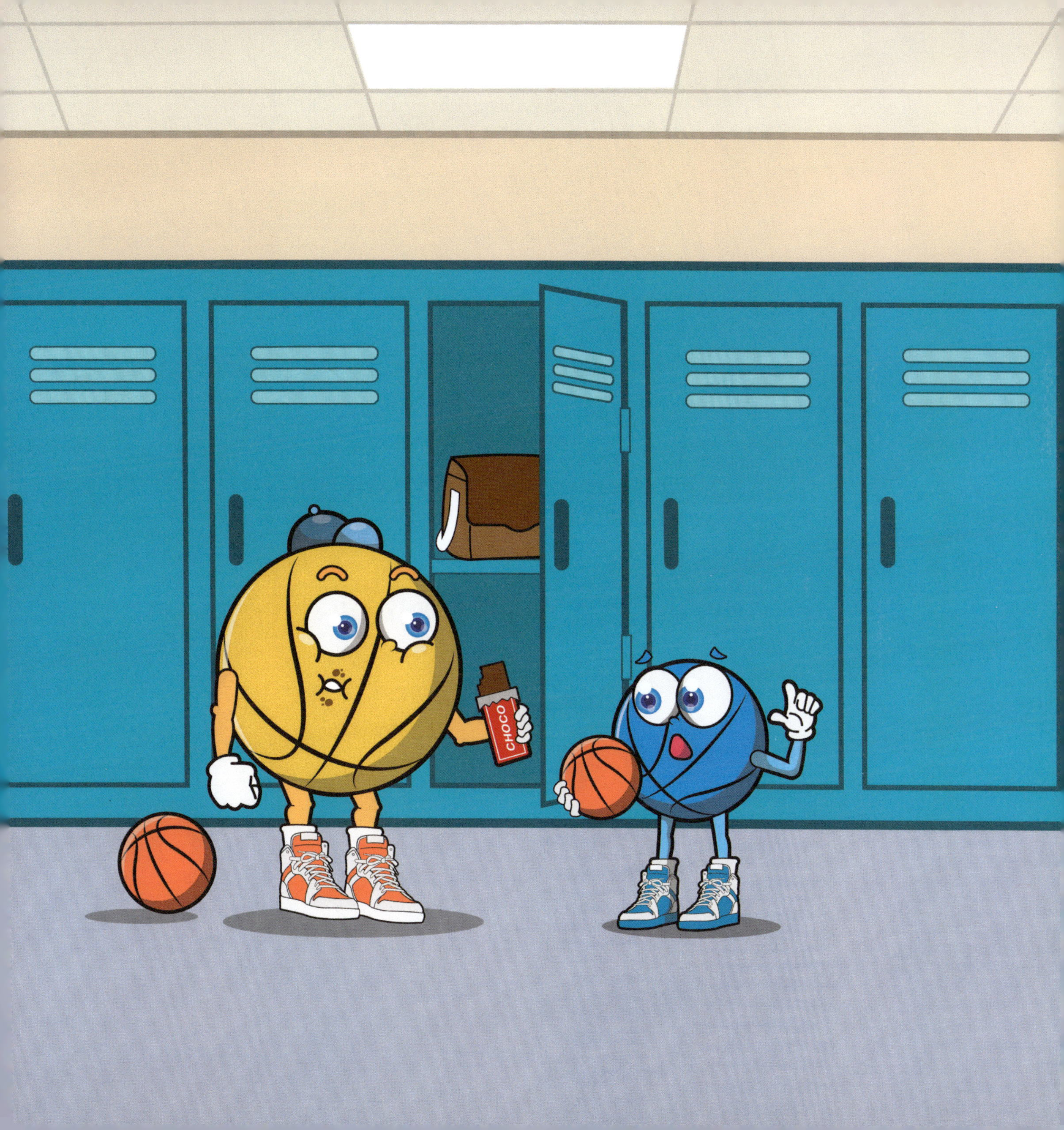
CHOCO

When the tryout started, Junk Food Baller had a surge of energy and felt great during the warm-up as he made all his shots in the lay-up line.

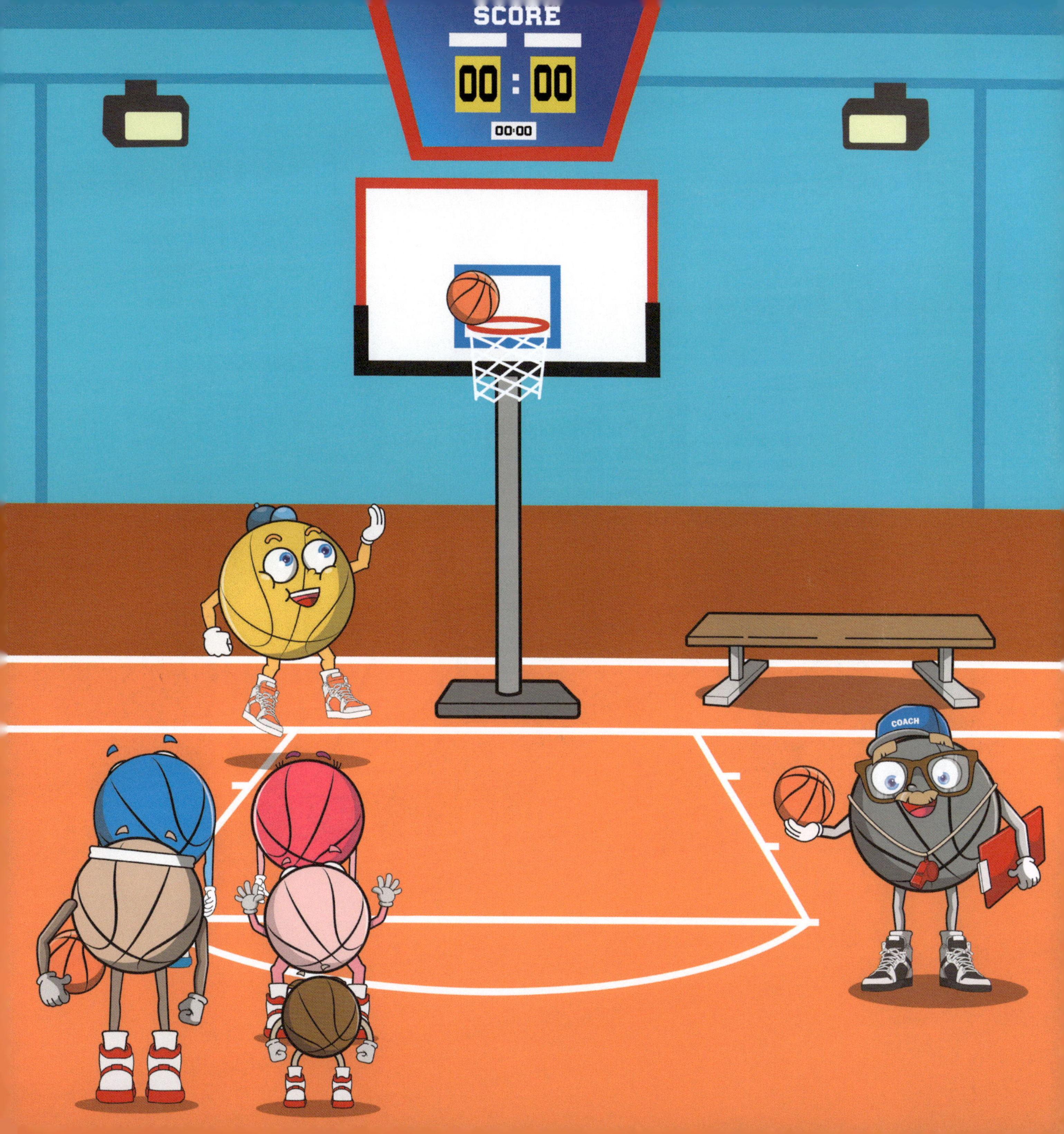
SCORE
00 : 00
00:00
COACH

But, after the second drill, Junk Food Baller started to feel his energy slipping away.

He began missing shots and struggling to keep up with his friends when they ran sprints.

Coach Swish asked him if he was ok, and he said yes, he needed a snack for more energy.

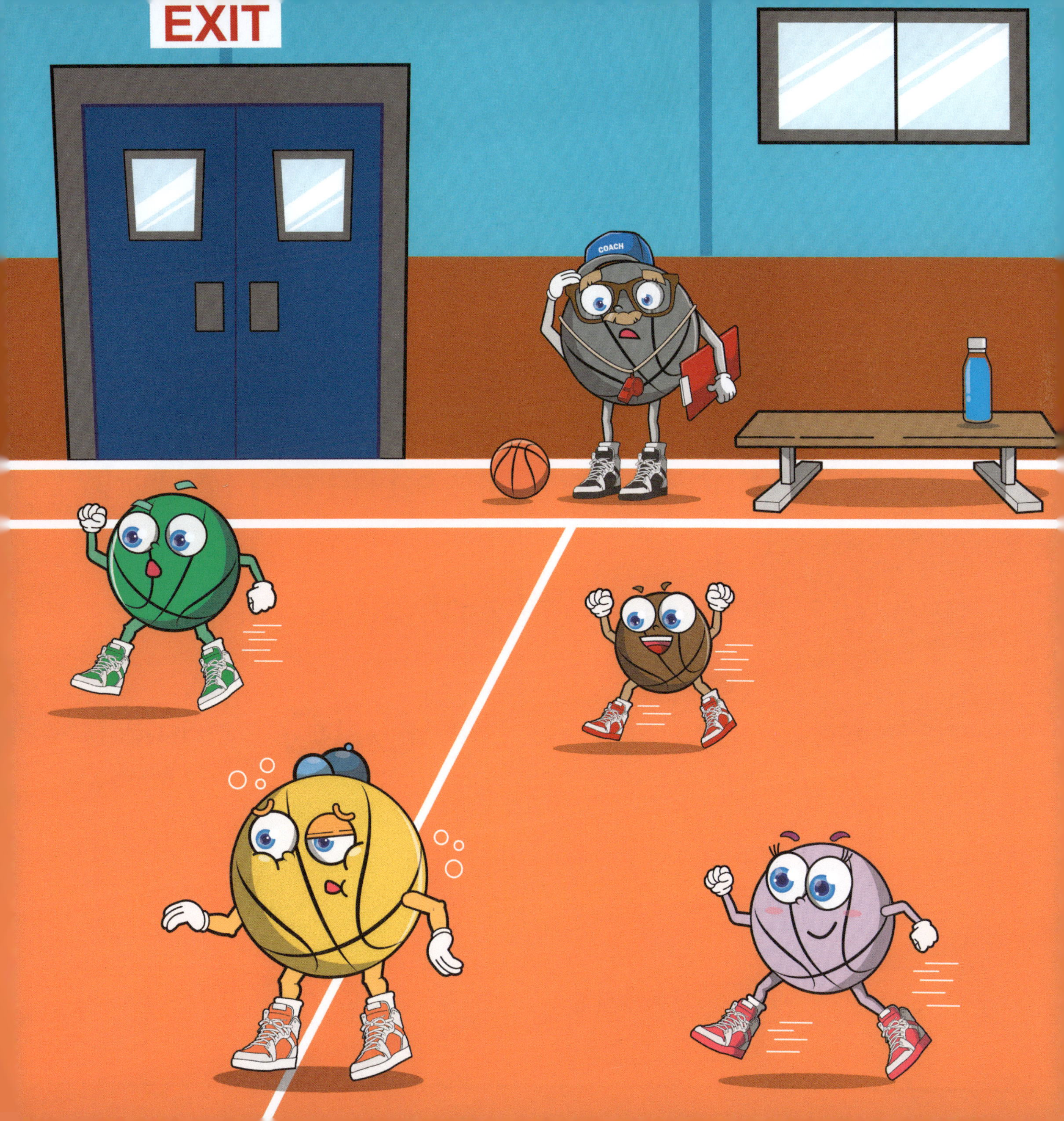
EXIT
COACH

At the first water break, Junk Food Baller felt like he had no energy left, so he ran to his bag, grabbed a mouthful of candy, and washed it down with a sugary sports drink to try and make himself feel better.

HOOPVILLE SCHOOL GYM

Junk Food Baller jumped back into the practice feeling more energy, but after a few minutes of scrimmaging, he felt even worse. He couldn't keep up with the game's pace, missed easy shots, and asked to be taken out of the game because he felt sick. Coach Swish looked worried.

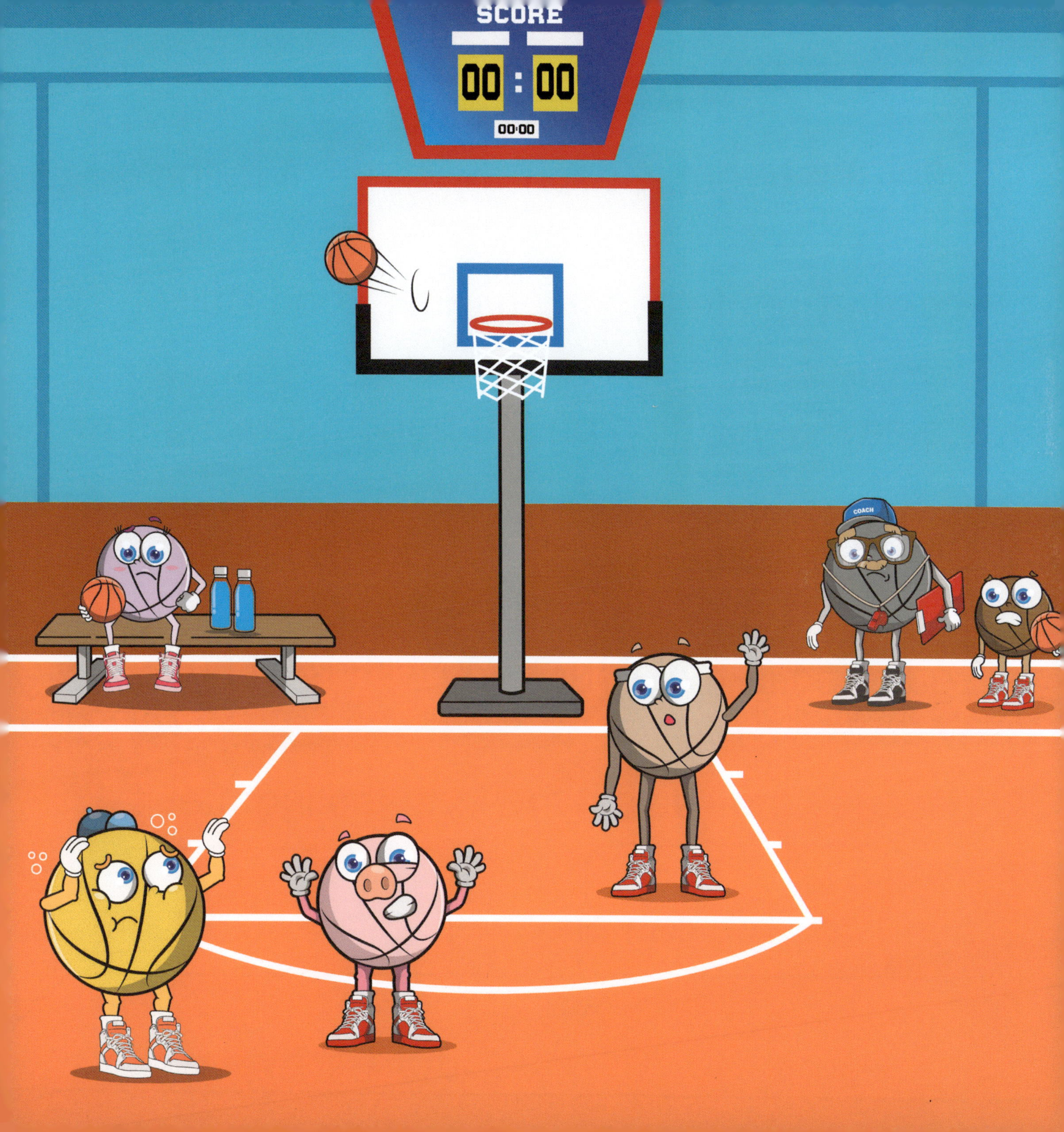
SCORE
00 : 00
00:00
COACH

After the tryout, Coach Swish went to the locker room to check on Junk Food Baller. He saw him sitting on the bench, looking sad. Coach Swish told him, "To excel in basketball, you need to fuel your body with healthy foods because they give it the long-lasting fuel it needs so you can play well.

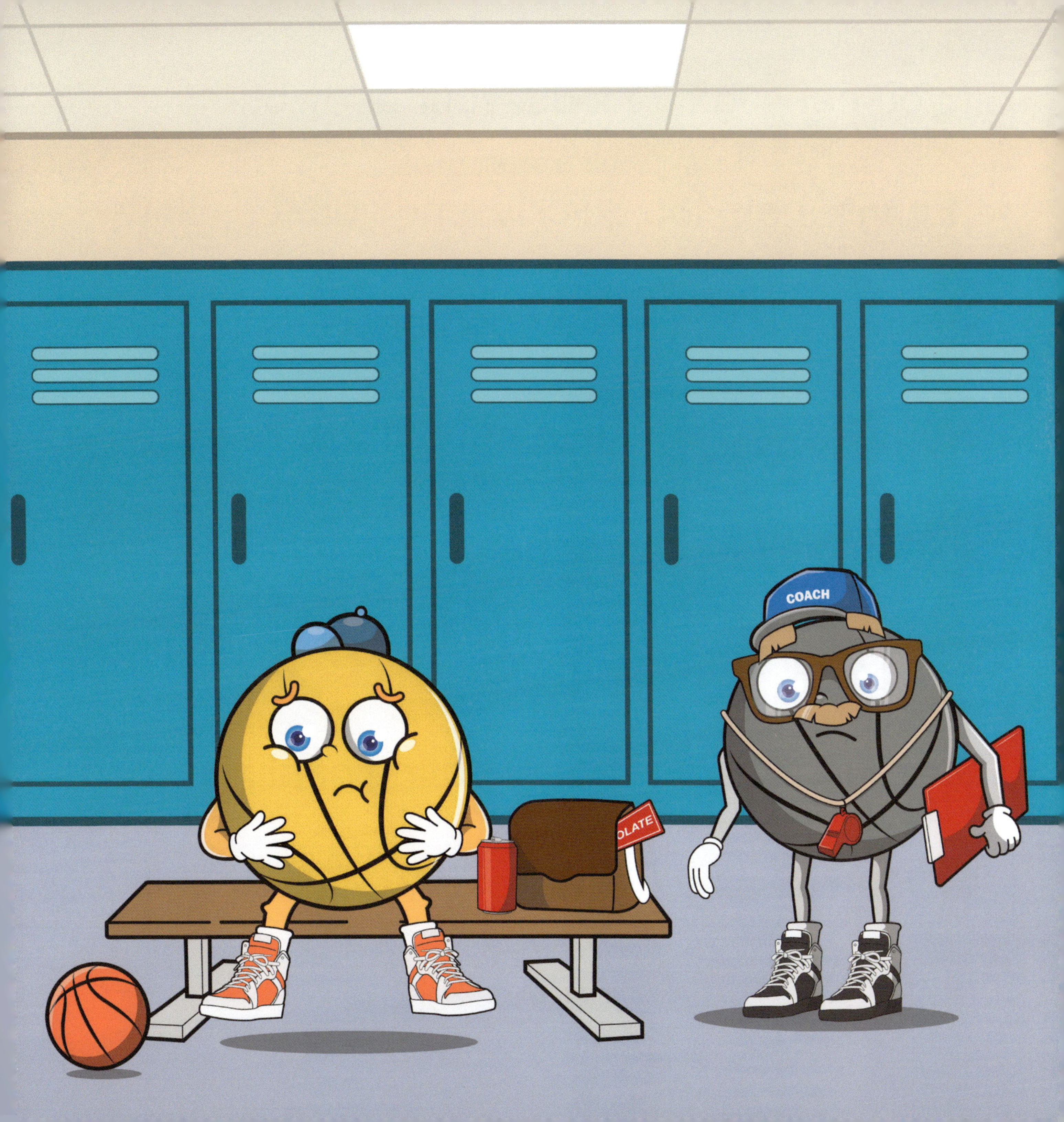
COACH
OLATE

If you eat sugary foods, your body burns through them too quickly, and you feel slow and unwell. You are a good basketball player. We need you on the team, but you need to be able to play for more than a few minutes without running out of energy.

Do you think you can try eating healthier foods so you can play on the team?

Junk Food Baller nodded yes.

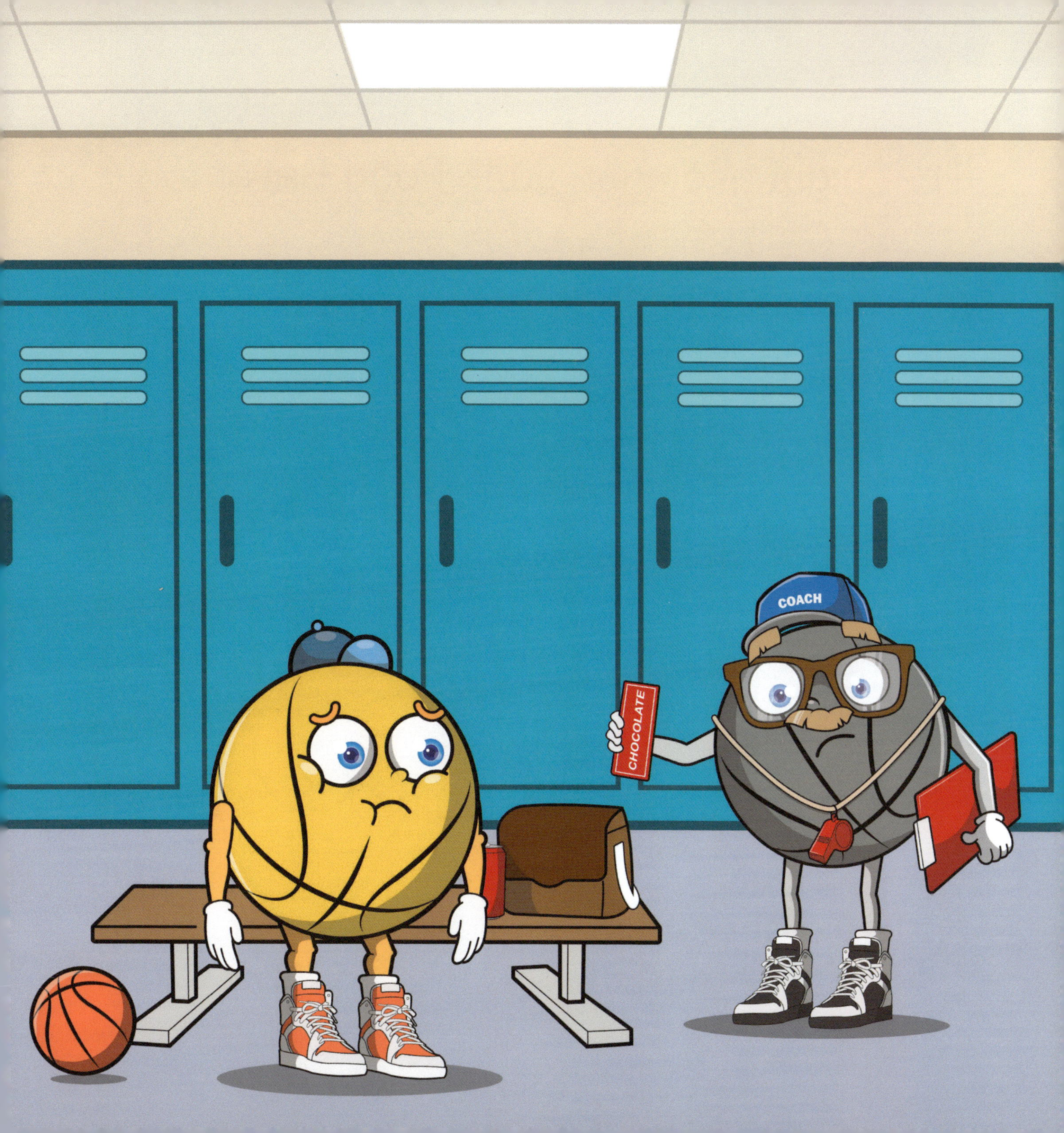
COACH
CHOCOLATE

That night at dinner, Junk Food Baller told his mom what happened at the tryout.

Feeling disappointed but determined, Junk Food Baller asked his mom to help him eat healthier.

She smiled and patted him on the shoulder and said of course.

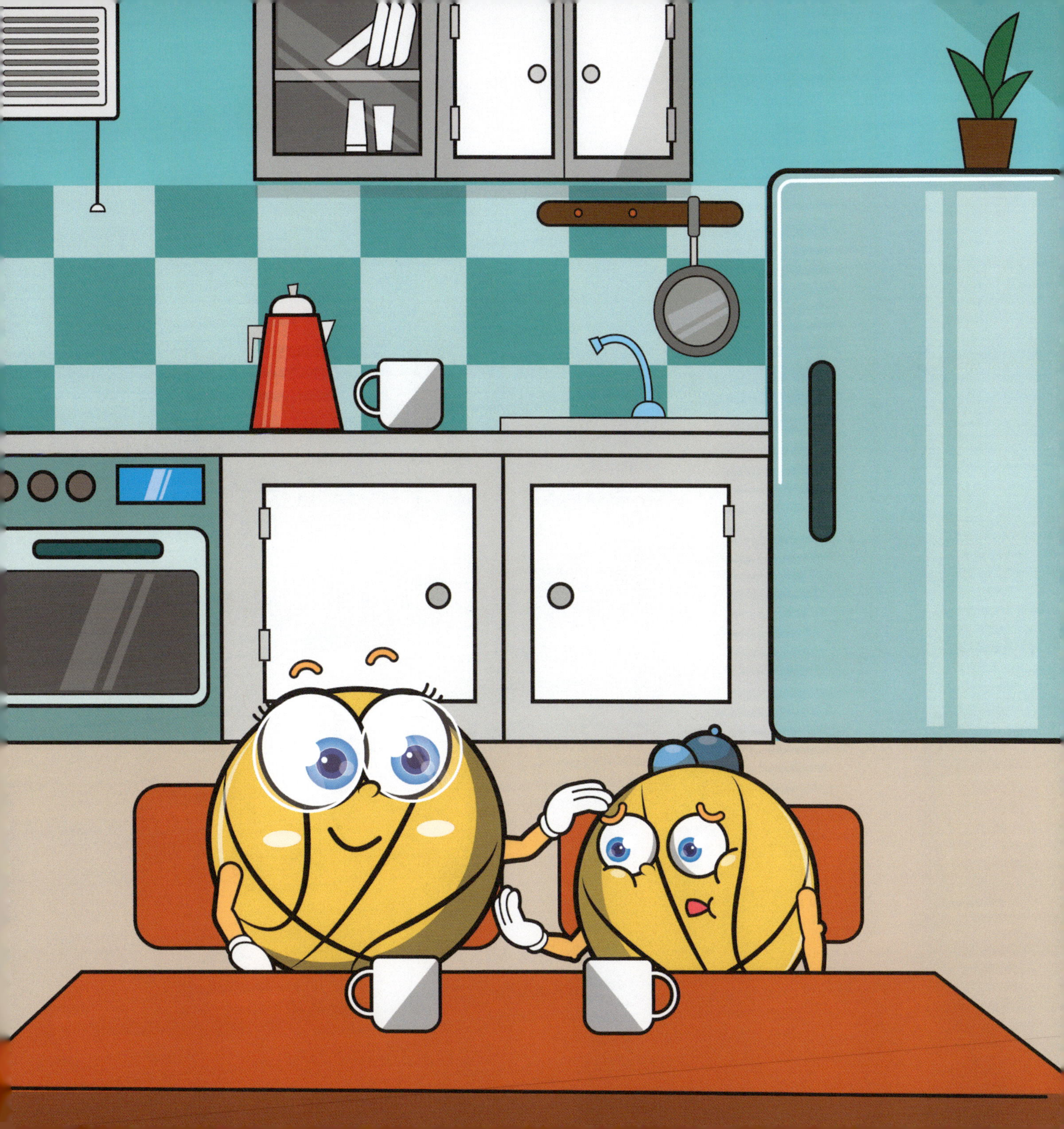

The next morning, Junk Food Baller's mom asked him what he wanted for breakfast.

He looked at the sugar cereal in the cupboard but remembered what the coach said.

Then he asked his mom to make him eggs and toast instead. His mom smiled at him.

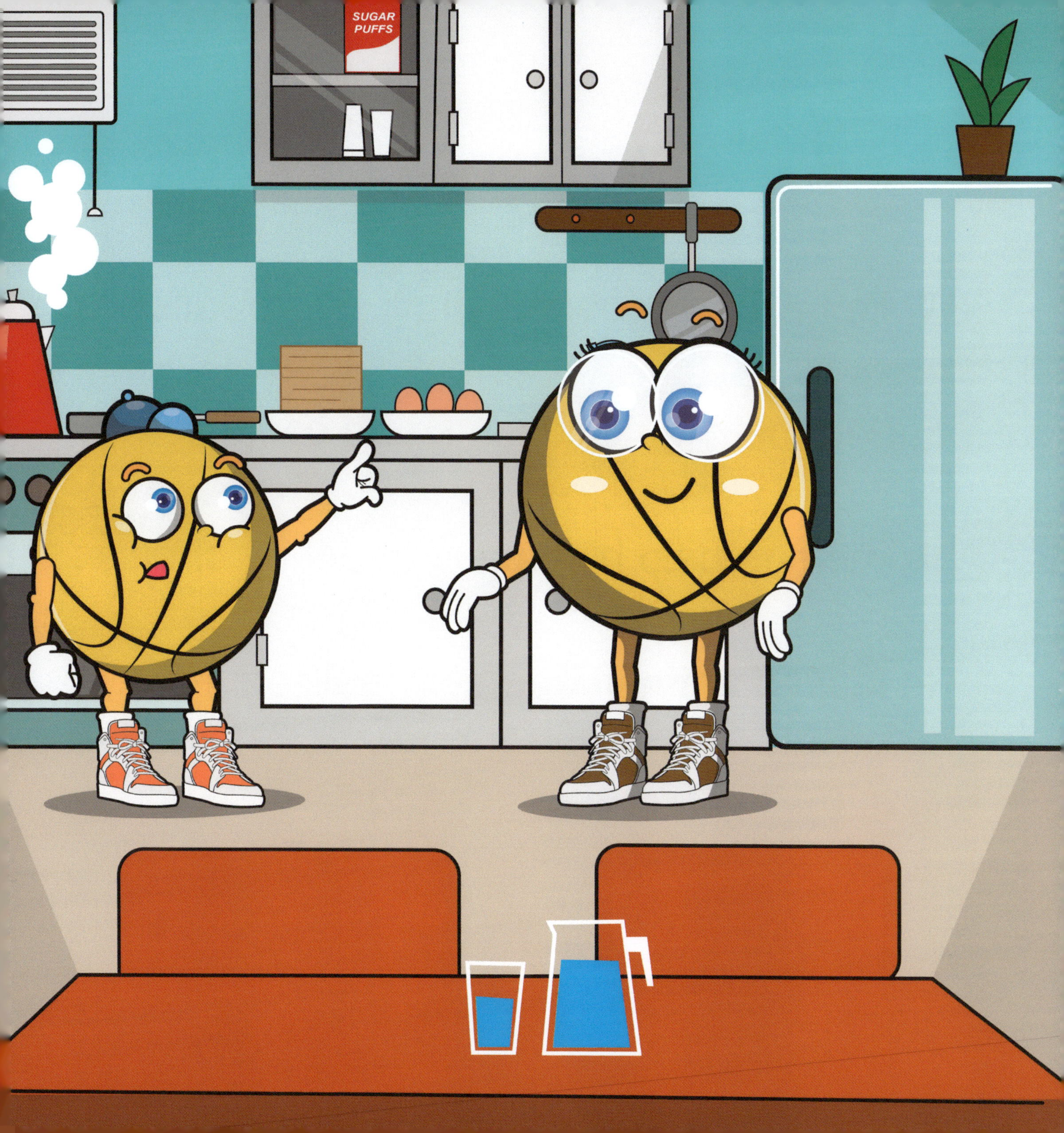
SUGAR
PUFFS

While his mom cooked, Junk Food Baller started making his lunch so he could ask his mom to help him make healthier choices. He looked at the fridge and realized he did not know what to make.

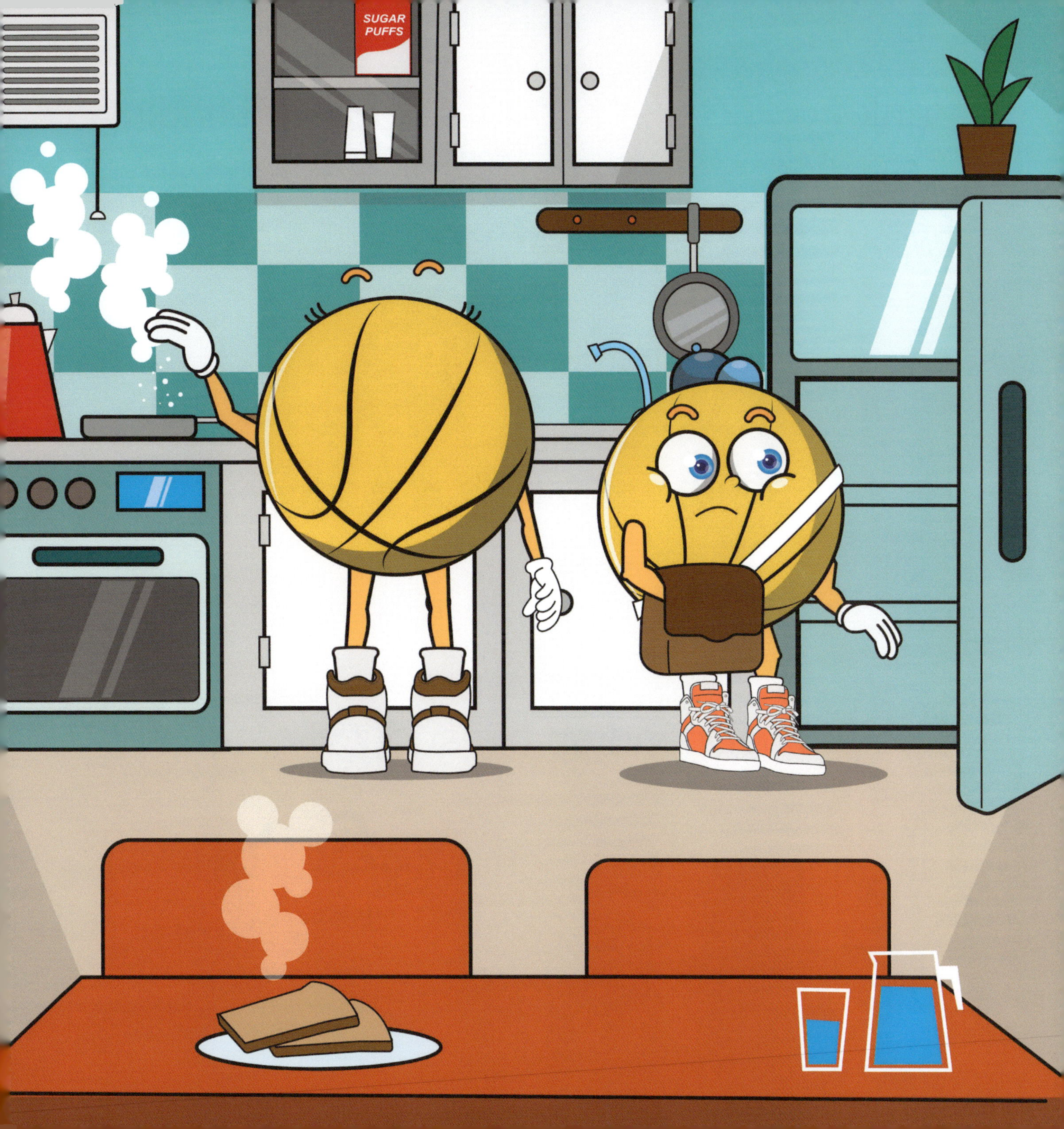
SUGAR PUFFS

Junk Food Baller's mom suggested finding two fruits, a vegetable, and a healthy sandwich for his lunch.

He was about to zip it up when his mom put a cookie into his bag, too.

She put her hand on his shoulder and told him that snacks in moderation were ok if most of his food was healthy.

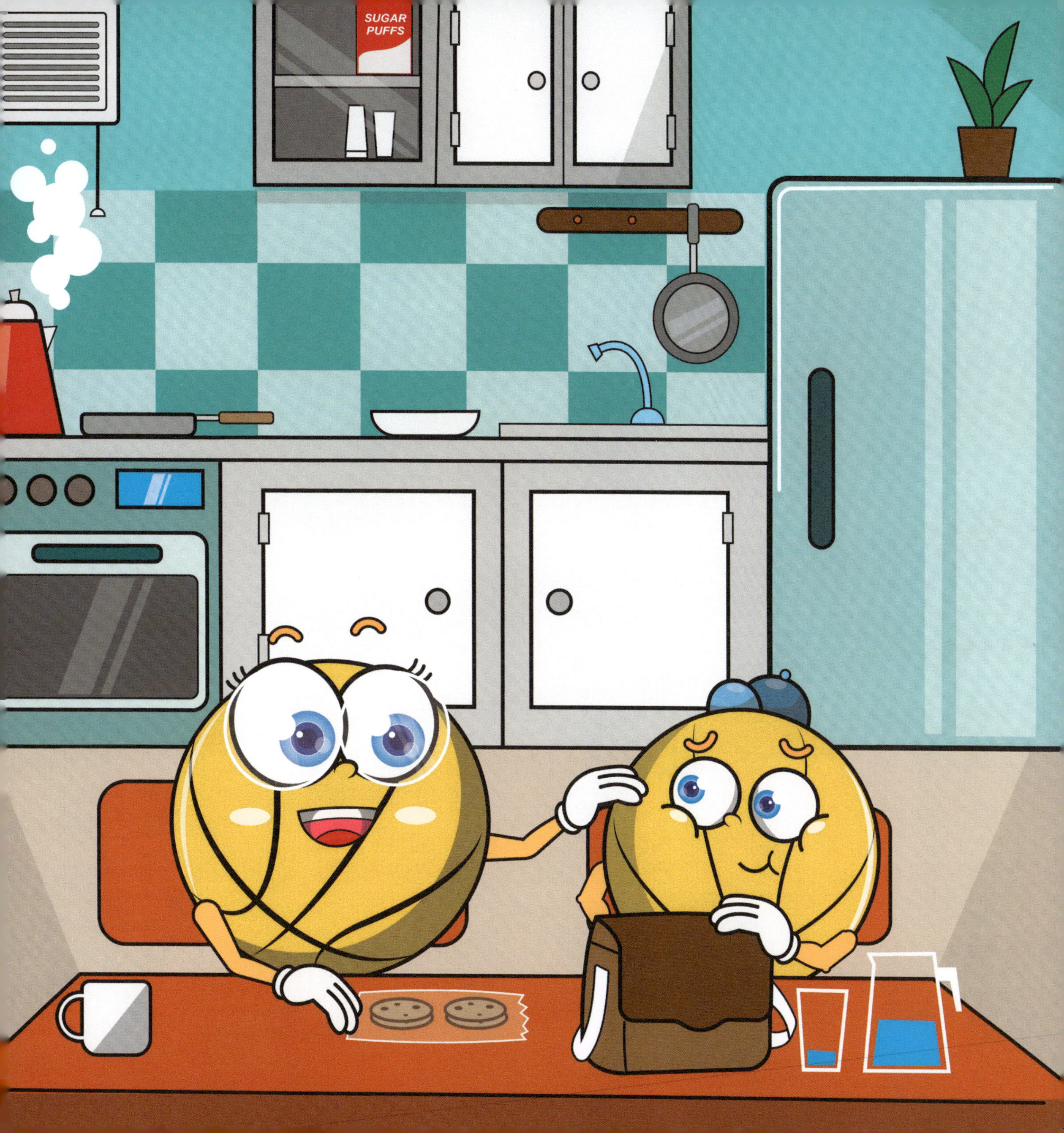
SUGAR
PUFFS

At the tryout after school, Junk Food Baller felt full of energy.

He arrived at the court fueled by nutritious foods and ready to give it his all.

His friends cheered as he played really well the whole time as Coach Swish watched.

HOOPVILLE SCHOOL GYM

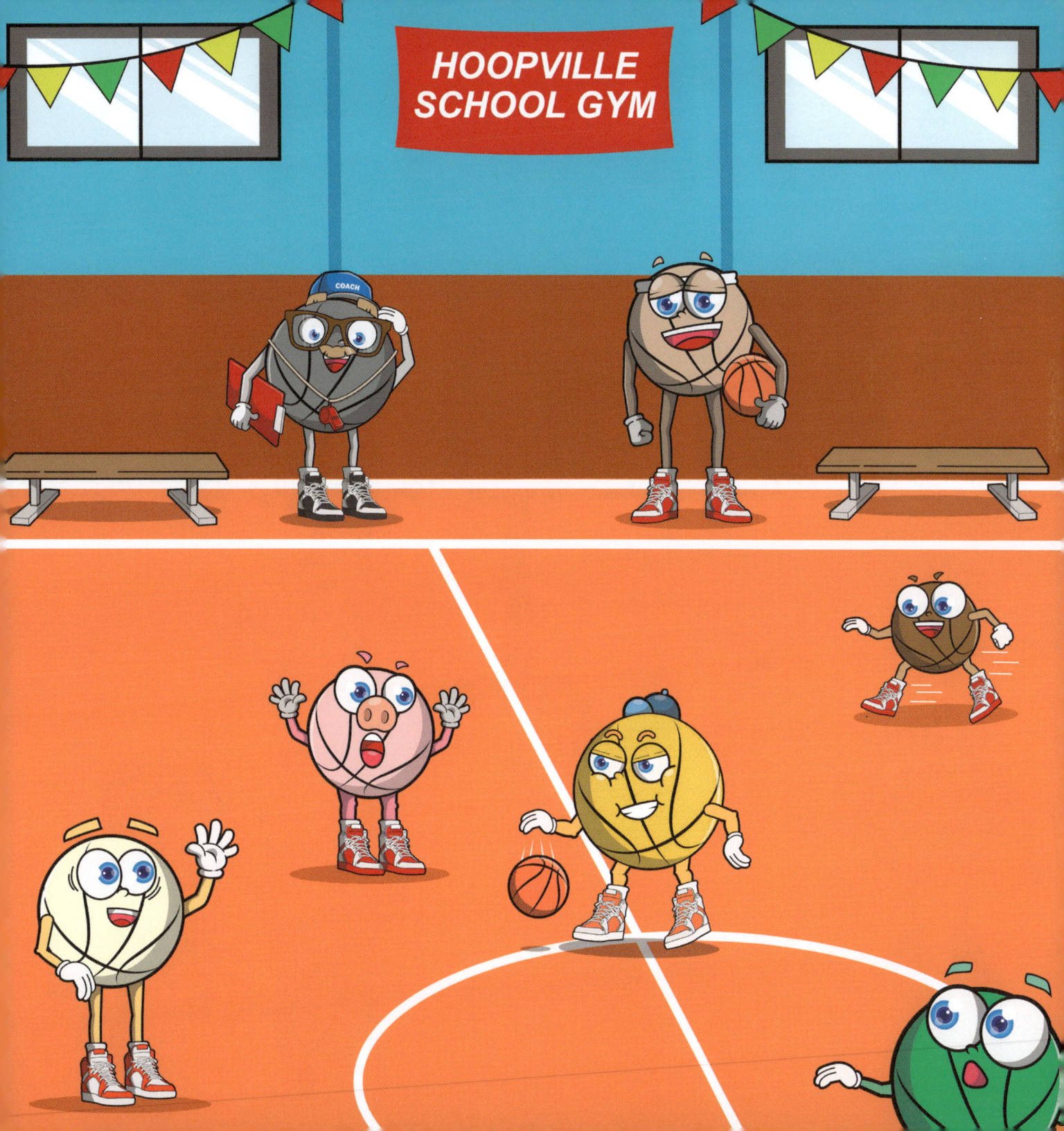

When the team list was posted, Junk Food

Baller's name was at the top of the list.

He was so excited and felt proud of his

healthier choices that day

EXIT

BASKETBALL TEAM:
JUNK FOOD BALLER
ROOKIE BALLER
TALL BALLER
GIRL BALLER
HOG BALLER
EYE ROLL BALLER
GOGGLES BALLER
TINY BALLER

That night at bedtime, he told his mom all about the tryouts and how great he felt about the healthy food he packed.

His mom smiled proudly and told him they could go to the store together, and he could help her pick healthy foods for the week.

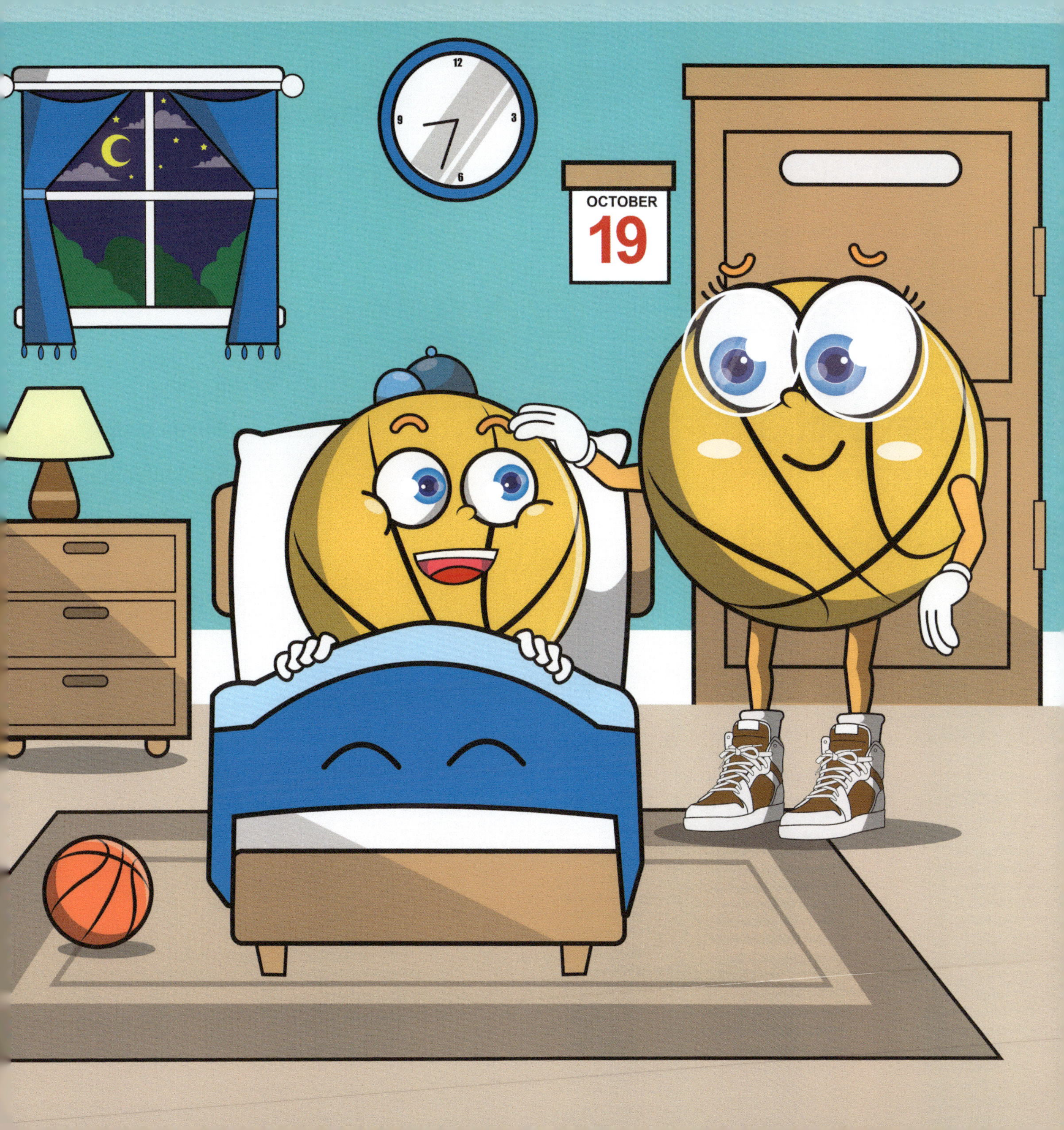
OCTOBER
19

As Junk Food Baller closed his eyes, he imagined himself hitting the game-winning shot at the championships.

He decided that to achieve his dream of becoming a basketball star, he needed to fuel his body with nutritious food, one healthy choice at a time.

Questions To Ask Your Child After Reading The Book

What is Junk Food Baller's big dream?

Why did Junk Food Baller's mom suggest he eat a healthy breakfast on the day of the tryouts?

What did Junk Food Baller eat instead of a healthy breakfast on the day of the tryouts?

How did Junk Food Baller feel during the tryout after eating sugary foods?

What did Coach Swish advise Junk Food Baller about his eating habits?

About The Author

Stephanie Rudnick is a mother, a writer, a motivational speaker, and the founding owner of Elite Camps, one of the largest basketball organizations of its kind in Canada.

Once a high-level player, she now helps athletes develop their on-court skills while ensuring that they, their parents, and their coaches all understand how the lessons learned on-court can prepare them for success in life.

Stephanie lives in Ontario with her husband, David, and their three sons.

Click the link below to be notified when I release the next Lil Baller book & download a free coloring sheet for your little baller.
https://lilballerbooks.com/

A Word By The Author

If you enjoyed this book, please take a moment to leave a review on Amazon, as your kind feedback is very appreciated and so very important to help spread the word about books designed to support families on their sports journey. Thank you so very much for your support.

Click this link to leave a review

https://linktr.ee/stephanierudnick

THANK YOU..

Printed in Great Britain
by Amazon